Smithsonian

Exploring the

Rhode Island

Colony

by Robin S. Doak

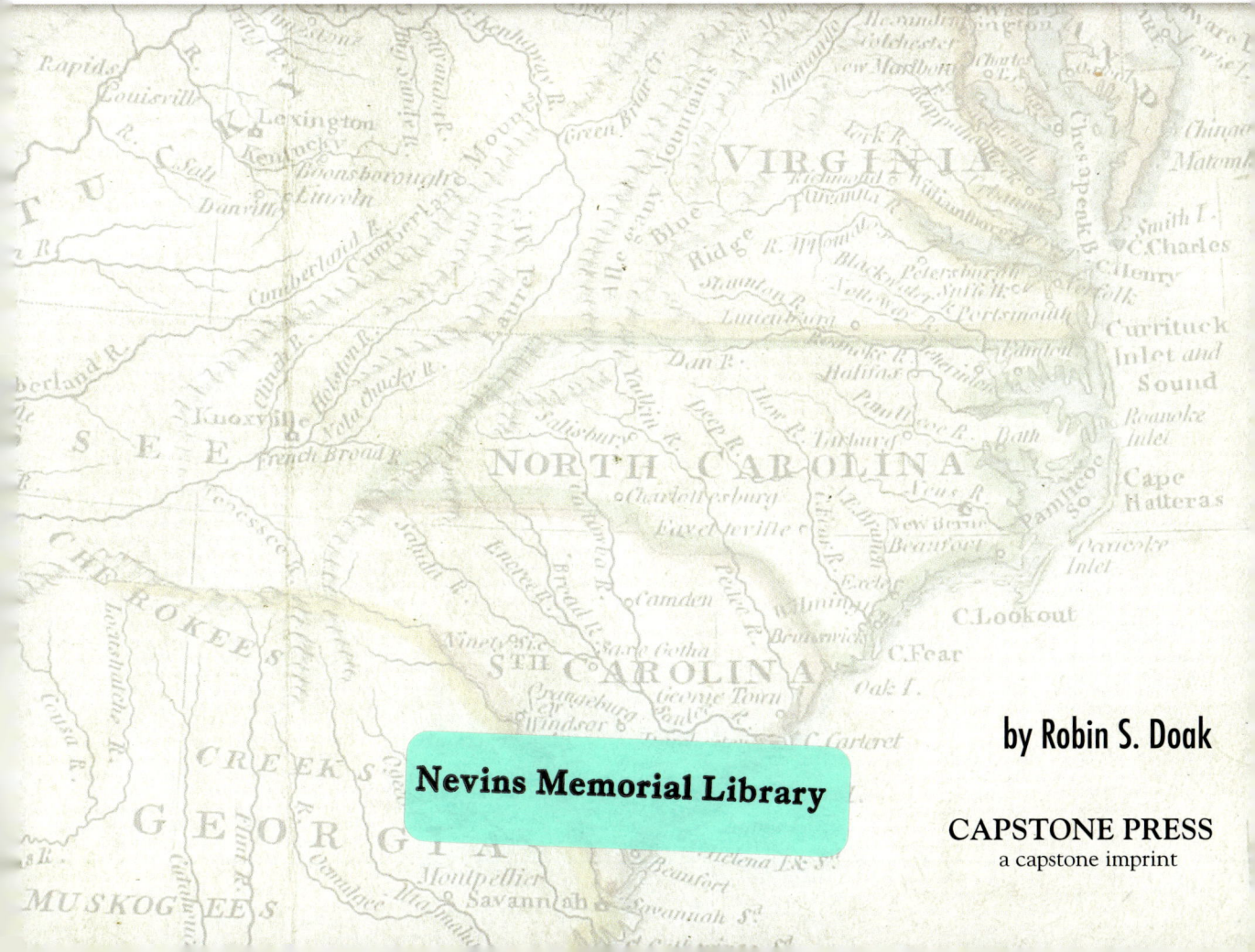

CAPSTONE PRESS
a capstone imprint

Smithsonian books are published by Capstone Press,
1710 Roe Crest Drive, North Mankato, Minnesota 56003
www.capstonepub.com

The name of the Smithsonian Institution and the sunburst logo are registered trademarks of the
Smithsonian Institution. For more information, please visit www.si.edu.

Library of Congress Cataloging-in-Publication Data
Names: Doak, Robin S. (Robin Santos), 1963– author.
Title: Exploring the Rhode Island colony / by Robin S. Doak.
Description: North Mankato, Minnesota: Capstone Press, 2017. | Series:
   Smithsonian. Exploring the 13 colonies | Includes bibliographical
   references and index. | Audience: Ages 8–11. | Audience: Grades 4–6.
Identifiers: LCCN 2016002547| ISBN 9781515722311 (library binding) | ISBN
   9781515722441 (pbk.) | ISBN 9781515722571 (ebook (pdf))
Subjects: LCSH: Rhode Island—History—Colonial period, ca.
   1600–1775—Juvenile literature.
Classification: LCC F82 .D629 2017 | DDC 974.5/02—dc23
LC record available at http://lccn.loc.gov/2016002547

Editorial Credits
Gina Kammer, editor; Richard Parker, designer; Eric Gohl, media researcher;
Kathy McColley, production specialist

Our very special thanks to Stephen Binns at the Smithsonian Center for Learning and Digital Access for
his curatorial review. Capstone would also like to thank Kealy Gordon, Smithsonian Institution Product
Development Manager, and the following at Smithsonian Enterprises: Christopher A. Liedel, President;
Carol LeBlanc, Senior Vice President; Brigid Ferraro, Vice President; Ellen Nanney, Licensing Manager.

Photo Credits
Alamy: Niday Picture Library, 10, Pictorial Press Ltd, 34; Capstone: 4, 28; Corbis: Bettmann, 25, 33;
David R. Wagner: 40; Getty Images: Archive Photos, 14, Kean Collection, 13, 16, 26, Print Collector,
32; Granger, NYC: 31; The Image Works Archives: 19; Library of Congress: 7, 11, 38 (left); Newscom:
Danita Delimont Photography/DanitaDelimont.com/Angel Wynn, 12, World History Archive, 38
(right); North Wind Picture Archives: cover, 5 (all), 9 (all), 15, 18, 20, 21, 22, 23, 24, 27, 29, 35, 36, 37, 39;
Providence City Archives: 17; Wikimedia: Public Domain, 30, 41

Design Elements: Shutterstock

Printed and bound in the USA.
009669F16

Table of Contents

RHODE ISLAND

Introduction:
The 13 Colonies

The history of the United States of America begins with the founding of 13 English colonies in North America. A **colony** is a settlement where people from another country have made their homes but still remain subject to laws of their original homeland. These early outposts along the eastern coast of North America would serve as the foundation for the United States.

Europeans Find a "New World"

In 1492 Christopher Columbus sailed from Spain and discovered land unknown to Europeans. The rulers of Portugal, England, France, and the Netherlands were quick to send their own explorers. Soon the countries had staked out claims throughout South, Central, and North America. Europeans called this the "New World" even though Native American tribes had been living there for thousands of years.

Rhode Island was the smallest of the original 13 Colonies.

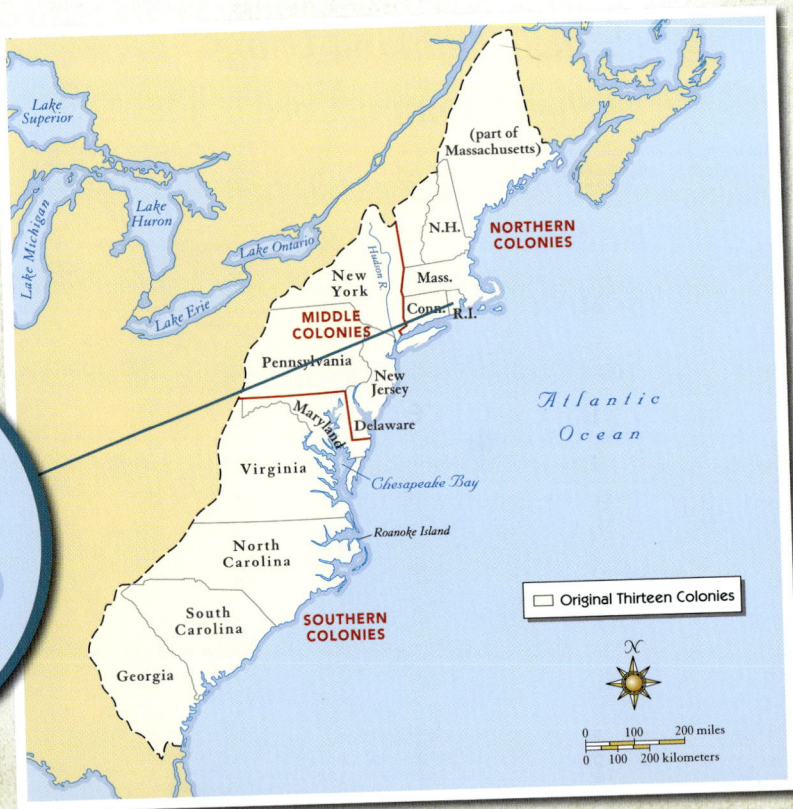

R.I.

Lake Superior
Lake Michigan
Lake Huron
Lake Ontario
Lake Erie
Hudson R.
(part of Massachusetts)
N.H.
NORTHERN COLONIES
New York
Mass.
Conn.
R.I.
MIDDLE COLONIES
Pennsylvania
New Jersey
Delaware
Maryland
Atlantic Ocean
Virginia
Chesapeake Bay
Roanoke Island
North Carolina
South Carolina
SOUTHERN COLONIES
Georgia

☐ Original Thirteen Colonies

N

0   100   200 miles
0   100   200 kilometers

England Carves Out Its Claim

Beginning with a voyage made by John Cabot in late 1497, England claimed much of the eastern coast of North America. But the claims were worthless if England did nothing with this new territory. About a century passed before England made plans to strengthen those claims by starting settlements.

colony—a place that is settled by people from another country and is controlled by that country

The 13 Colonies

Virginia was the first English colony in what is now the United States. In 1607 John Smith and about 100 English men and boys founded Jamestown in Virginia. This was the first permanent English settlement in North America. Colonies to the north of Virginia soon followed. By 1732 the American Colonies stretched nearly the entire length of the East Coast of the present-day United States. The only exception was Florida, which was controlled by the Spanish.

Starting a New Life

The people in the 13 Colonies shared some common bonds. For one thing, they were all subject to the laws and decisions of the English king. More importantly, those who came to the colonies all shared a common goal. Each new settler hoped to create a better life in the New World. Some of the first colonies were founded by people hoping to openly practice their religions in peace. Other colonies were founded to make money for the land's owners.

The Original 13 Colonies

The first permanent European settlement in each colony:

Virginia	1607	Delaware	1638
Massachusetts	1620	Pennsylvania	1643
New Hampshire	1623	North Carolina	1653
New York	1624	New Jersey	1660
Connecticut	1633	South Carolina	1670
Maryland	1634	Georgia	1733
Rhode Island	1636		

Each colony developed its own unique character. For example, a colony's climate and landscape affected the crops colonists grew and how they made a living. Some colonies were more successful than others, and grew more quickly as a result.

The first English colonists were all subjects of England's King James I.

Did You Know?

The area of metropolitan Los Angeles is about four times as large as all of Rhode Island.

The Smallest Colony

Providence Plantations, as Rhode Island was first known, was founded by Roger Williams in 1636. Rhode Island was one of the colonies in the region that John Smith named New England. The New England colonies also included Massachusetts, New Hampshire, and Connecticut.

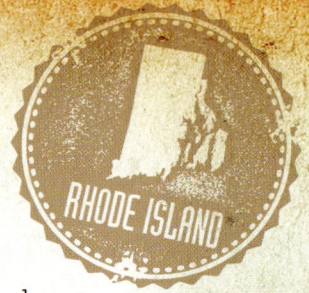

Rhode Island was the smallest of all the colonies. It was bordered by the two **Puritan** colonies of Massachusetts and Connecticut. To the south was the Atlantic Ocean. Rhode Island's location played an important role in its development. People from the two neighboring colonies helped populate Rhode Island. Its ports on the Atlantic made it a major center of trade throughout the Colonial period.

The Most Accepting Colony

Settlers seeking religious freedom founded the Rhode Island Colony. They also wanted people of other religions to be able to practice their faiths freely. This acceptance of religions caused people in nearby colonies to look upon Rhode Island with anger. But in 1663 the king guaranteed that no one in Rhode Island could be punished for religious beliefs.

> *"… noe person within the sayd colonye … shall bee … punished … or called in question, for any differences in opinione in matters of religion …"*
>
> —Charter of Rhode Island and Providence Plantations, July 15, 1663

Rhode Island quickly grew into an important Colonial center of trade and business.

Puritan—a follower of a strict religion common during the 1500s and 1600s; Puritans wanted simple church services and enforced strict morals

Chapter 1:
Native Peoples of Rhode Island

   Before the arrival of Europeans, the land now known as Rhode Island was home to several Native American groups. The largest group was the Narragansett tribe. Other tribes included the Niantics, Nipmucks, and Wampanoags. The tribes shared a common language group, known as Algonquian. In all, thousands of native people lived in the area.

Canonicus (second from left) was the leader of the Narragansett people during the early 1600s. This is an artist's idea of what Canonicus might have looked like.

When the first European settlers arrived, Canonicus was the most powerful Narragansett chief in Rhode Island. Rhode Island's founder, Roger Williams, described him as being "very sour." Canonicus accused Williams of bringing a **plague** to his people. However, the chief slowly came to trust the Englishman.

Massasoit, a chief of the Wampanoag people, befriended Williams and other early settlers in Rhode Island and Massachusetts. He attended the first Thanksgiving feast with the Pilgrims in 1621.

In this 19th century engraving, Massasoit is shown with his warriors and early New England settlers.

plague—a disease that spreads quickly and kills most people who catch it

Life in a Native Village

Native villages in Rhode Island were usually made up of several families who were related to each other. The families lived in separate wigwams clustered together around a central, open area. The wigwam was a hut with a rounded top. It was made of branches draped with animal hides, tree bark, or grass mats.

Rhode Island tribes survived by hunting and farming. Men used spears, traps, and bows and arrows to hunt deer, moose, turkey, and other game. Women grew crops of beans, corn, and squash. They also gathered berries and plants for food and medicine.

The Narragansetts and other Rhode Island tribes lived in wigwams, huts that were easily set up and taken down.

An artist has imagined what a Wampanoag man looked like in this engraving. He is shown with a spear and bow.

Each year tribes migrated between summer and winter camps. In the summer, they lived near the sea. Men fished while women dug for clams and collected **mussels**. In the winter tribes moved inland, away from the cold sea air.

Tribes were not always friendly toward one another. The Narragansetts and the Wampanoags were enemies, often battling for territory and hunting rights. The Narragansetts also fought the Pequots of Connecticut and the Mohawks of New York.

The arrival of Europeans in the 1500s and 1600s began a decline for the native people in Rhode Island. Diseases brought by explorers and fishermen wiped out large numbers of native people. Later, a terrible war would result in the deaths of thousands.

mussel—a type of shellfish with two joined shells

Chapter 2:
Founding a New Colony

RHODE ISLAND

In 1524 Italian explorer Giovanni da Verrazzano explored the eastern coast of North America. When he visited Rhode Island, Verrazzano and his crew gave the Wampanoags gifts of bells, mirrors, and other trinkets.

Verrazzano liked what he saw in Rhode Island. In a letter he called the natives the "goodliest people." And he wrote that the land he explored was "pleasant as is possible to declare."

In 1614 Dutch explorer Adriaen Block set up trading posts in the area. He hoped to work with the native people of Rhode Island, exchanging European goods for animal furs. Block also named an island off the coast of Rhode Island for himself: Block Island.

Verrazzano and other explorers were welcomed to Rhode Island by the Wampanoags and other tribes.

> *"This is the goodliest people, and of the fairest conditions that we have found in this our voyage."*
>
> —Giovanni da Verrazzano, in a letter dated July 8, 1524

New diseases were introduced to North America with the arrival of early European traders and later with the arrival of colonists.

European visitors to the area brought diseases with them such as **smallpox** and measles. The native people had no defenses against these new diseases. In 1616, an **epidemic** wiped out around a thousand Wampanoag people in the region.

English Colonists Arrive

In 1630 people from England founded the Massachusetts Bay Colony. Settlers in Massachusetts soon ventured into Rhode Island. Like the explorers before them, they traded with the Narragansetts and other tribes.

Did You Know?

It is uncertain where the name Rhode Island came from. Giovanni da Verrazzano compared Rhode Island to the Mediterranean Island of Rhodes, so some historians believe that's where the name came from. Others believe Adriaen Block named the area for its red clay. "Roodt Eylandt" means "red island" in Dutch.

smallpox—a disease that spreads easily from person to person, causing chills, fever, and pimples that scar

epidemic—an infectious disease that spreads quickly through a community or group

A Providence in the Wilderness

Roger Williams was a Puritan clergyman who first settled in Massachusetts. Williams openly challenged the strict church leaders. He also believed that the colonists should pay native tribes for any land they took. Williams, a friend to the local tribes, learned to speak native languages and treated the natives fairly.

Williams' outspokenness and **radical** views angered leaders in Massachusetts. He wanted the government to be run separately from the church. In 1635 he was put on trial for those views. Colonial leaders decided that he should be sent back to England. But instead Williams fled the colony in January 1636 and traveled south to the area that would become Rhode Island. The Wampanoag people took Williams in and gave him shelter for the winter.

Roger Williams (1603?–1683)

Born in London, England, Roger Williams was the son of a merchant. As a young man, Williams became a clergyman. Facing arrest for his religious beliefs, Williams traveled to the New World in 1631 in search of greater religious freedom. But he quickly learned that he would not find this freedom in Massachusetts. Williams then founded Rhode Island in 1636, even serving as the colony's first president. He died in Providence in 1683.

In the spring Williams and a group of six families from Massachusetts began building Rhode Island's first settlement. He called it Providence Plantations. The Narragansett people gave the land to Williams. Later, Williams paid the native people for more land in the area.

Critical Thinking with Primary Sources

The deed that Roger Williams and the Narragansetts signed is a tattered but important document. Why do you think this document was unusual for its time? Why do you think Roger Williams took the time to write this document? How do you think the deed affected relations between the natives and the English colonists?

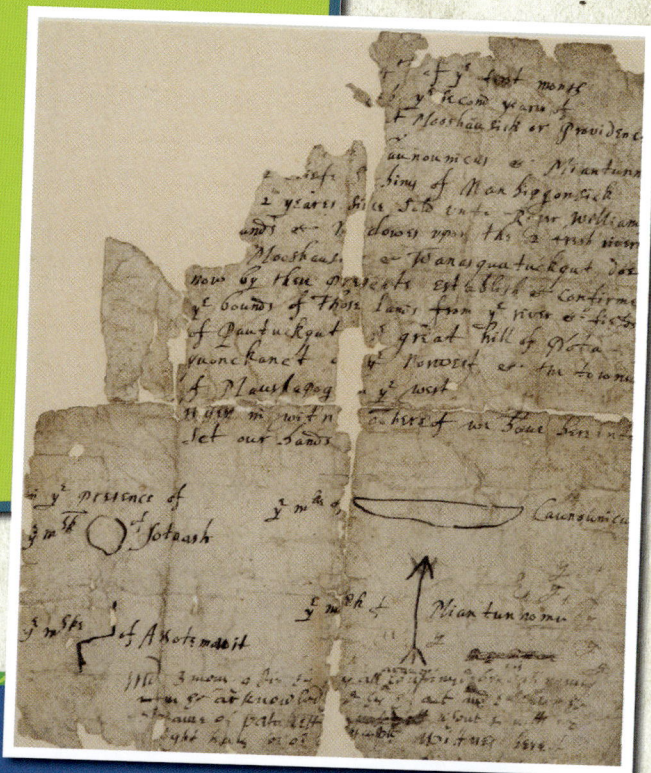

Did You Know?

Roger Williams called the place he came to in Rhode Island "Providence" after "God's merciful providence" brought him there. The word *Providence* means a God who provides for people or the protection of a providing God.

radical—extreme compared to what most people think or do

Three New Towns

Williams and the other colonists in Providence gathered at town meetings and decided together what the colony's new rules should be. The most important decision was that people in Rhode Island could practice any religion they chose.

Rhode Island soon attracted other settlers looking for religious freedom. Anne Hutchinson arrived in 1638 and helped found the town of Portsmouth. Like Williams, Hutchinson had been kicked out of Massachusetts for her religious views.

In 1639 William Coddington split off from the settlers in Portsmouth. He and a few of his followers moved a short distance away and founded Newport. Warwick, the fourth of Rhode Island's original towns, was founded in 1642.

Only treaties with the Native Americans allowed the Rhode Islanders to own the land they settled. They did not have a royal **charter** from England to give them official ownership. Massachusetts and Connecticut joined together to form a military force, but they did not include the settlers of what they called "**Rogue's** Island." To protect themselves the Rhode Island settlers united under one government. Finally in 1644 England's **Parliament** gave the settlers their first charter.

RHODE ISLAND

Anne Hutchinson (1591–1643)

Anne Hutchinson arrived in Massachusetts in 1634 with her husband and their 15 children. Hutchinson soon found herself at odds with the Puritan leaders of the colony. She settled in Rhode Island, but when her husband died in 1642, she decided to move on. Hutchinson next settled in the Dutch colony of New Netherland. The following year, Hutchinson and many of her children were killed when Native Americans raided their home. In 1922, a statue of this courageous spiritual leader was erected in front of the Massachusetts State House.

William Coddington moved out of Portsmouth and built his house in Newport.

After the towns joined together as one colony in 1644, they agreed to a central government. The colonists of Rhode Island formed a democratic government in the mid-1640s. In those days, however, "democratic" meant that only free white males were allowed to vote.

> Rhode Island was declared "Democraticall; that is to say, a Government held by ye free and voluntarie consent of all ... of the free Inhabitants."
>
> —an excerpt from Rhode Island's General Assembly, May 1647

This new government did not last long because the towns preferred governing themselves. But in 1654 Roger Williams was appointed president of the Rhode Island Colony. Over the next three years, he worked hard to unite the colony under one government.

charter—an official document granting permission to set up a new colony, organization, or company

rogue—a person who causes trouble or is dishonest

Parliament—Great Britain's lawmaking body

Chapter 3:
Life in Early Rhode Island

As the years passed, the little settlements grew. In Providence the first log cabins were replaced by larger, sturdier homes made of stone and wood. Each home had two stories. The upper story was for sleeping. The central feature of the lower story was a huge fireplace for cooking and for warming the house.

The first families had few belongings in their homes. They had necessary furniture such as chairs, a table, and bedrolls for sleeping. Pots and other cooking items were important, as were candles for lighting the little homes. Later, colonists would add glass to their windows and other more decorative items.

Early log homes in Rhode Island had dirt floors and **thatched** roofs.

Colonists held town meetings to make decisions.

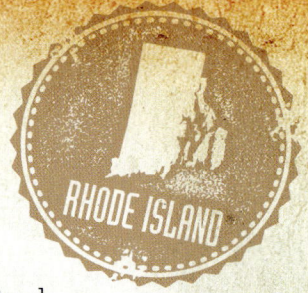

Making a Living in Rhode Island

The earliest colonists in Providence received plots of land. They grew corn, squash, beans, and other foods. They learned how to grow these new crops with the help of local tribes. The first colonists also planted fruit trees and kept livestock. They raised sheep, chicken, cows, and horses. They built fences to keep livestock away from the crops.

Families of settlers supported themselves with their own farm products. The extras were traded to other settlements and colonies. Before long, the colony was shipping wood, meat, and dairy products as far away as the Caribbean.

RHODE ISLAND

Farming was the first important industry in Rhode Island.

Newport Trades

In Newport colonists turned to trade and fishing. Many of the first settlers had been merchants in Massachusetts, and they brought their money and knowledge with them. Newport soon became a center of trade throughout the colonies.

The shipping and fishing industries gave work to shipbuilders, barrel makers, rope makers, and other craftsmen. By the mid-1600s, Newport had become one of the most important towns in all the colonies.

Life in Colonial times was not easy. People worried constantly about starvation and disease. Young people were especially affected by illness. As many as four out of every 10 children in 17th-century New England died before becoming adults.

Children played an important role in the Colonial family. From a very young age, they were expected to help out. In the morning children got up early and worked for most of the day. Boys helped their fathers tend crops and livestock. Girls helped their mothers gather vegetables, prepare food, spin thread, and wash clothing.

Children were expected to work alongside their parents farming and doing other chores, such as churning butter.

Newport had a public school in 1640, but most children were taught to read and write at home by their mothers. The Bible was the most important book they studied. Boys were also taught basic math. As they got older, they might learn a trade—like carpentry or **blacksmithing**—that would support them as adults.

In the mid-1700s housewives set up schools in their own homes for neighboring children. These schools were known as "dame schools." Here, boys and girls were taught reading and writing, along with subjects such as dancing and French. Girls were also taught arts such as embroidery.

Children learn to read and write at a dame school set up in a Colonial home.

blacksmith—a person who makes and fixes things made of iron

Bad Times

By 1660 Rhode Island's population had grown to about 1,500. But the colony was still threatened. Massachusetts and Connecticut continued to claim land within the colony. To settle the issue, King Charles II granted Rhode Island a new charter in 1663. The charter gave Rhode Island religious freedom and clear borders to try to put an end to threats from the neighboring colonies.

In 1675 fighting broke out between the Wampanoags and colonists in Massachusetts and Connecticut. The colonists had executed three Wampanoags for committing murder, which made the natives angry. The Wampanoags also wanted their land back. Rhode Island and many of the Narragansetts tried to stay out of the fighting. But this didn't stop men from the two nearby colonies from entering Rhode Island and killing nearly a thousand Narragansetts living there.

Metacom (1639?–1676)

Metacom, a Wampanoag chief, was the son of Massasoit. Born around 1639, he was known to the colonists as King Philip. At first Metacom traded peacefully with the colonists in Massachusetts and Rhode Island. He even wore English clothes bought in Boston. But Metacom realized that Massachusetts colonists had stolen land from his people. He was determined to take this land back. Metacom was killed in August 1676, bringing the bloody war with his name to an end.

Both colonists and natives committed acts of great cruelty during King Philip's War.

Soon New England was at war. During what was known as King Philip's War, Providence and Warwick were nearly destroyed in attacks by the Narragansetts. By the time the war ended in 1676, thousands of Native Americans had been killed. Many survivors were enslaved.

Chapter 4:
A Growing Colony

After King Philip's War, the Rhode Island Colony continued to grow and succeed. The colony's well-known religious acceptance attracted new settlers. By the early 1700s, the colony was home to Anglicans, Baptists, Calvinists, Catholics, Jews, and Quakers. Jews and Catholics, however, were not allowed to vote because they were not followers of Protestant religions.

In 1708 Rhode Island took its first **census**. At that time, the population of the colony numbered more than 7,100. In less than 50 years, that number climbed to more than 40,400. Most people lived in Providence and Newport, and more towns were also established.

Critical Thinking with Primary Sources

Rhode Island got its first seal in 1664, a year after King Charles II granted the colony a new royal charter. Why do you think colonists chose the word *Hope*? What does the anchor on the seal symbolize? If you were designing a new seal for your town, what would it look like?

HOPE

Rhode Island and its neighbors became more friendly during the early 1700s. Around this time **stagecoach** service between Rhode Island and Boston began. In addition, there was a weekly post for mail from Boston, New York, and other Colonial centers.

A stagecoach travels along the Boston Post Road carrying mail from Boston to Rhode Island.

census—an official count of the number of people in an area
stagecoach—a horse-drawn vehicle for carrying people and goods

29

A Maritime Metropolis

By the early 1700s, Newport was the business and political center of Rhode Island. It would also become one of the colony's first capital cities. Newport continued to rely on the sea as its source of wealth. In the 1700s whaling became important to the town. Its deep-water port for ships and tolerance for rule breakers also made it a safe haven for pirates.

One pirate, Thomas Tew, captured several ships in the Indian Ocean. He and his crew wanted to spend their treasure in the Caribbean. But a storm blew them off course, and they headed to Newport in Rhode Island instead. They knew it was a good place to sell their treasure on the **black market**.

Newport and Slavery

Newport was a center of the Colonial slave trade. Newport merchants owned ships that were part of the **Triangular Trade**. The ships carried sugar and molasses from the West Indies to Rhode Island, where they were used to make rum. The rum was then shipped to Africa and traded for kidnapped African men and women.

Did You Know?

Newport's Thomas Tew became known as "the Rhode Island Pirate."

Thomas Tew (left) tells his pirating stories to the governor of New York.

RHODE ISLAND

By the 1700s Newport was a busy and wealthy port city.

The enslaved people were shipped to the West Indies to work on **plantations**. The two-month trip from Africa to the Americas was called the Middle Passage. Conditions on board the ships were horrible, and many slaves died on the voyage.

Other enslaved people were brought back to the colonies. They were forced to work on plantations in the South, as well as in Northern Colonies like Rhode Island. By the mid-1700s, thousands of Africans had come to the colonies on ships made in Newport.

Did You Know?

"The Ocean State" is Rhode Island's official nickname. Although the state is small, it has more than 400 miles of coastline.

black market—a system of buying or selling stolen or illegal goods
Triangular Trade—the exchange of sugar, rum, and slaves among the West Indies, the American Colonies, and Africa
plantation—a large farm where crops are raised by the people who live there

Colonial Culture

Newport was also a center of Colonial culture during the 1700s. Some of the finest mansions in New England were built there. Wealthy colonists filled their big houses with furniture imported from Europe. They shopped for the latest clothing fashions at the many stores in town. Artisans and craftsmen easily found work in Newport.

Mansions such as this one were owned by the richest colonists.

The Narragansett Pacer was a type of strong, fast horse that was bred in Rhode Island for racing. Today the Narragansett Pacer is extinct.

One of the biggest attractions for visitors and residents alike was horse racing. Rhode Island was the only New England colony that allowed this sport. On racing days crowds of people flocked to South Kingstown to watch the riders compete for a silver cup. Many of the horses were Narragansett Pacers, which were bred in Rhode Island.

The Narragansett Planters

Newport wasn't the only center of wealth in Rhode Island. South of Providence was the Narragansett Country. There, rich farmers owned large plantations. These landowners were known as the Narragansett Planters.

Farmers grazed livestock, including cattle, sheep, pigs, and horses. In the good soil, they grew wheat, corn, tobacco, and other crops. Meat, dairy products, fruits, and vegetables were sent by cart and boat to Newport. There, Narragansett goods were shipped to other colonies as well as to England and other places.

Slavery in Rhode Island

At first farmers in the region kept indentured servants to work on their plantations. Indentured servants were men and women who signed a contract to work for a certain amount of time for one master. In exchange the master paid for the servants to come to the colonies from Great Britain.

Most slaves lived and worked on plantations in the Narragansett Country.

By the early 1700s, the servants had been almost completely replaced by African and Native American slaves. The Narragansett Country was one of the few regions in the North where large numbers of slaves were held. The owner of a large plantation might have as many as 40 slaves working for him.

In 1774 Rhode Island lawmakers passed a law that banned people from bringing slaves into the colony. However, the last of Rhode Island's slaves would not be free until 1859.

Slaves in Colonial mansions replaced the indentured servants.

Chapter 5:

From Colony to State

In 1733 Great Britain began placing taxes on some items that were shipped into the colonies. The first item to be taxed was molasses. Later, taxes were placed on sugar, stamps, newspapers, glass, paper, tea, and even playing cards.

Rhode Island merchants were upset by the taxes, and some refused to pay. They began **smuggling** taxed goods into the colony. In 1765 Britain created the Stamp Act, which required colonists to purchase a stamp for all printed documents. Rhode Island joined with the other colonies to issue a formal protest to the king over the Stamp Act. Rhode Island's Governor Samuel Ward announced that he would not punish colonists who disobeyed the act.

Critical Thinking with Primary Sources

Can you find clues to the colonists' views on taxes in this newspaper? What do you think the box in the top right corner was for? Do you think everyone agreed with this paper's viewpoint?

The TIMES are Dreadful Doleful Dismal Dolorous, and DOLLAR-LESS.

of the STAMP

An Emblem of the Effects of the STAMP O! the fatal Stamp

Adieu Adieu to the LIBERTY of the PRESS.

Thursday, October 31. 1765

NUMB 1195

THE

PENNSYLVANIA JOURNAL;

AND

WEEKLY ADVERTISER.

EXPIRING: In Hopes of a Resurrection to LIFE again.

I am sorry to be obliged to acquaint my readers that as the Stamp Act is feared to be obligatory

deliberate, whether any methods can be found to elude the chains forged for us, and escape the insupportable slavery, which it is hoped, from the last representation now made

hind Hand, that they would immediately discharge their respective Arrears, that I may be able, not only to support myself during the Interval, but be better prepar-

The burning of the *Gaspee* was one of the first serious acts of violence against the British.

Banding Together

Colonists in Rhode Island came together to oppose the new taxes. In 1764 Newport colonists fired cannons at a British ship trying to seize the vessel of a local smuggler. Another time, Providence residents attacked and beat a tax collector.

In Rhode Island and other colonies, men formed Sons of Liberty groups to oppose the British taxes. They held meetings under trees that they called "Liberty Trees." The Sons of Liberty sometimes threatened Stamp Act agents or burned **effigies** of them in the streets. Great Britain responded by sending more troops to Newport and other Colonial centers to keep the peace.

In 1772 Rhode Island's anger at Great Britain turned to violence. On the night of June 9, the Sons of Liberty rowed out to the *Gaspee*. The *Gaspee* was a British ship that was stuck on a sandbar off the coast of Warwick. The ship's crew had been trying to end smuggling in Rhode Island. The colonists captured the crew, then set the *Gaspee* on fire.

smuggle—to secretly and illegally bring items into or out of an area
effigy—a dummy made to look like a hated person

War Begins

Finally, on April 19, 1775, the Revolutionary War began. That day, **Patriots** and British soldiers battled at Lexington and Concord in Massachusetts.

Three months later, British warships arrived in Newport's harbor. They set up **blockades**, preventing food and other supplies from getting to Rhode Island.

On May 4, 1776, Rhode Island became the first of the colonies to announce its independence from Britain. Two months later, representatives from Rhode Island attended the Second Continental Congress. There they signed the Declaration of Independence, officially breaking with Great Britain.

Two Rhode Island Patriots

Two Rhode Island locals became famous for their bravery during the Revolutionary War. **Nathanael Greene (1742–1786)** served as a general in the Continental army. Greene fought in many battles alongside George Washington. He earned fame by holding back British forces in South Carolina until the end of the war.

A Providence man, **Esek Hopkins (1718–1802)** was a sailor his entire life. During the war, he was chosen to be the first **commodore**, or chief commander, of the Continental navy. However, he did not always follow orders. Congress dismissed him from the navy, but he continued to serve the country in the Rhode Island General Assembly.

The Sons of Liberty defend a Liberty Tree from British soldiers. Providence's Liberty Tree was dedicated in July 1768.

Did You Know?

Rhode Island Independence Day is celebrated every May 4.

Patriot—a person who sided with the colonies during the Revolutionary War

blockade—a closing off of an area to keep people or supplies from going in or out

Rhode Island at War

Like most American colonists, Rhode Island residents suffered during the war. The British Army captured Newport in December 1776. The enemy would control Newport for three years. Buildings were burned, homes were destroyed, and colonists fled. The city was ruined by the revolution. The once thriving port was reduced to a small harbor. It would take many years for Newport to recover from the damage caused by the British occupation.

Many Providence residents worked together to support the war, collecting arms and other supplies. Men from throughout Rhode Island came to Providence to enlist in the Continental army. At home, women made fabric and sewed clothing, mittens, and socks for American soldiers.

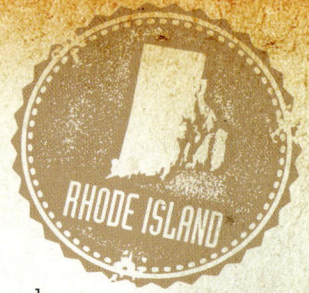

The 1st Rhode Island Regiment was made up of many African-American and Native American slaves.

The signing of the U.S. Constitution created the new nation's government.

When Rhode Island regiments needed more soldiers, the 1st Rhode Island Regiment allowed Native American and African-American slaves into its ranks. They were offered freedom in exchange for their service. Freed slaves also became soldiers. They fought their first battle, the Battle of Bloody Run Brook, in Rhode Island in 1778. They fought back three British attacks in the largest land battle in New England.

From Colony to State

The Revolutionary War officially came to an end in September 1783. A peace treaty was signed by Great Britain and the United States. It recognized the United States of America as an independent nation. Although Rhode Island had quickly embraced independence, it was not so eager to join the new nation. Rhode Islanders did not want to give up their hard-won independence to a national government.

In 1787 Rhode Island refused to send representatives to the **Constitutional Convention**. At this meeting men from the other former colonies wrote the U.S. Constitution, the foundation of the new national government. Finally on May 29, 1790, Rhode Island became the 13th state. It was the last of the original 13 Colonies to **ratify** the Constitution.

Constitutional Convention—the meeting during which a group of people wrote the Constitution of the United States
ratify—to formally approve

Timeline

1492 Christopher Columbus, sailing for Spain, reaches the Americas.

1524 Italian explorer Giovanni da Verrazzano reaches the coast of Rhode Island.

1607 John Smith helps found Jamestown, Virginia, the first permanent English settlement in the United States.

1614 Dutch explorer Adriaen Block names Block Island, off the coast of Rhode Island, for himself.

1616 An epidemic wipes out around a thousand Wampanoag people.

1635 Roger Williams is ordered to leave the Massachusetts Bay Colony.

1636 Rhode Island is founded by Roger Williams.

1638 Anne Hutchinson helps found Portsmouth on Aquidneck Island.

1639 William Coddington founds Newport, on the southern tip of Aquidneck Island.

1642 Warwick, the last of Rhode Island's four original settlements, is founded.

1644 Roger Williams visits England and receives a charter from Parliament.

1663 Rhode Island receives a new charter from King Charles II.

1675 King Philip's War wipes out most of Rhode Island's Native American population.

1733 Great Britain passes the first of several taxes that anger colonists.

1765 Rhode Island takes part in the Stamp Act Congress.

1772 Rhode Island colonists burn the British ship *Gaspee*.

1774 Rhode Island's legislature bans the importation of slaves into the colony.

1775 War breaks out between Great Britain and the American Colonies.

1776 On May 4, Rhode Island is the first colony to declare its independence from Great Britain. On July 4, the Declaration of Independence is adopted.

1779 The last British troops leave Rhode Island.

1783 Great Britain and the United States sign the Treaty of Paris, formally ending the Revolutionary War.

1787 Rhode Island refuses to send any representatives to the Constitutional Convention.

1790 Rhode Island is the last of the original 13 Colonies to ratify the Constitution.

Glossary

black market (BLAK MAR-kit)—a system of buying or selling stolen or illegal goods

blacksmith (BLAK-smith)—a person who makes and fixes things made of iron

blockade (blok-AYD)—a closing off of an area to keep people or supplies from going in or out

census (SEN-suhs)—an official count of the number of people in an area

charter (CHAR-tuhr)—an official document granting permission to set up a new colony, organization, or company

colony (KAH-luh-nee)—a place that is settled by people from another country and is controlled by that country

Constitutional Convention (kahn-stuh-TOO-shuh-nuhl kuhn-VEN-shuhn)—the meeting during which a group of people wrote the Constitution of the United States

effigy (EH-fuh-jee)—a dummy made to look like a hated person

epidemic (eh-puh-DEH-mik)—an infectious disease that spreads quickly through a community or group

mussel (MUHSS-uhl)—a type of shellfish with two joined shells

Parliament (PAHR-luh-muhnt)—Great Britain's lawmaking body

Patriot (PAY-tree-uht)—a person who sided with the colonies during the Revolutionary War

plague (PLAYG)—a disease that spreads quickly and kills most people who catch it

plantation (plan-TAY-shuhn)—a large farm where crops are raised by people who live there

Puritan (PYOOR-uh-tuhn)—a follower of a strict religion common during the 1500s and 1600s; Puritans wanted simple church services and enforced strict morals

radical (RAD-ik-uhl)—extreme compared to what most people think or do

ratify (RAT-if-eye)—to formally approve

rogue (ROHG)—a person who causes trouble or is dishonest

smallpox (SMAWL-poks)—a disease that spreads easily from person to person, causing chills, fever, and pimples that scar

smuggle (SMUHG-uhl)—to secretly and illegally bring items into or out of an area

stagecoach (STAYJ-kohch)—a horse-drawn vehicle for carrying people and goods

thatched (THACHD)—made of straw, hay, or leaves

Triangular Trade (try-AN-gyuh-lahr TRAYD)—the exchange of sugar, rum, and slaves among the West Indies, the American Colonies, and Africa

Critical Thinking Using the Common Core

1. How did colonists react to British taxes? (Key Ideas and Details)
2. How do the biography boxes help to support the text? What would the book be like without them? (Craft and Structure)
3. If Roger Williams had not been forced to leave the Massachusetts Bay Colony, do you think Rhode Island would be a state today? Why or why not? (Integration of Knowledge and Ideas)

Read More

Cunningham, Kevin. *The Rhode Island Colony.* New York: Children's Press, 2012.

Micklos, John, Jr. *The Making of the United States from Thirteen Colonies— through Primary Sources.* Berkeley Heights, N.J.: Enslow Publishers, 2013.

Pratt, Mary K. *A Timeline History of the Thirteen Colonies.* Minneapolis, Minn.: Lerner Publications, 2014.

Roza, Greg. *The Colony of Rhode Island.* New York: PowerKids Press, 2015.

Internet Sites

FactHound offers a safe, fun way to find Internet sites related to this book. All of the sites on FactHound have been researched by our staff. Here's all you do:
Visit *www.facthound.com*
Type in this code: 9781515722311

www.FACTHOUND.com

Super-cool stuff!

Check out projects, games and lots more at
www.capstonekids.com

Source Notes

Page 8, callout quote: "Charter of Rhode Island and Providence Plantations—July 15, 1663." The Avalon Project: Lillian Goldman Law Library. Accessed January 12, 2016. http://avalon.law.yale.edu/17th_century/ri04.asp#1.

Page 11, line 3 quote: James D. Knowles. *Memoir of Roger Williams, the Founder of the State of Rhode-Island*. Boston: Lincoln, Edmands and Co., 1834, p. 130.

Page 14, line 6, callout quote: *Collections of the New York Historical Society for the Year 1809*. Vol. 1, New York: I. Riley, 1811, pp. 25, 54.

Page 15, fact box: Howard M. Chapin. "How Rhode Island Got Its Name." RI.gov, Accessed November 30, 2015. http://sos.ri.gov/library/history/name/.

Page 17, fact box: William R. Staples. *Annals of the Town of Providence from Its First Settlement to the Organization of the City Government, in June 1832*. Vol. 5, Collections of the Rhode-Island Historical Society. Providence, R.I.: Knowles and Vose, 1843, p. 30.

Page 19: callout quote: "1647: Acts and Orders (Rhode Island)." Liberty Fund, Inc. Last modified April 10, 2014. http://oll.libertyfund.org/pages/1647-acts-and-orders-rhode-island.

Regions of the 13 Colonies

Northern Colonies	Middle Colonies	Southern Colonies
Connecticut, Massachusetts, New Hampshire, Rhode Island	Delaware, New Jersey, New York, Pennsylvania	Georgia, Maryland, North Carolina, South Carolina, Virginia
land more suitable for hunting than farming; trees cut down for lumber; trapped wild animals for their meat and fur; fished in rivers, lakes, and ocean	the "Breadbasket" colonies—rich farmland, perfect for growing wheat, corn, rye, and other grains	soil better for growing tobacco, rice, and indigo; crops grown on huge farms called plantations; landowners depended heavily on servants and slaves to work in the fields

Select Bibliography

Arnold, Samuel Greene. *History of Rhode Island*. 2 vols. Providence, RI: Preston & Rounds, 1899.

Carson, Cary, Ronald Hoffman, and Peter J. Albert, eds. *Of Consuming Interests: The Style of Life in the Eighteenth Century*. Charlottesville, V.A.: University of Virginia Press, 1994.

Earle, Alice Morse. *Home Life in Colonial Days*. Stockbridge, Mass.: Berkshire Traveller Press, 1974.

Fitts, Robert K. *Inventing New England's Slave Paradise: Master/Slave Relations in Eighteenth-Century Narragansett, Rhode Island*. New York: Garland Publishing, Inc., 1998.

"History of Rhode Island." RI.gov. 2015. Accesssed November 30, 2015. http://www.sos.ri.gov/library/history/.

James, Sydney V. *Colonial Rhode Island: A History*. New York: Charles Scribner's Sons, 1975.

LaFantasie, Glenn W. "Liberty for the Soul." American History Magazine 42 no. 1, (2007): 24–29.

Langdon, William Chauncy. *Everyday Things in American Life, 1607–1776*. New York: Charles Scribner's Sons, 1937.

Maier, Pauline. *Ratification: The People Debate the Constitution, 1787–1788*. New York: Simon & Schuster, 2010.

PBS. "Religious Freedom: The Trial of Anne Hutchinson." *The American Experience: Wayback—Stand Up for Your Rights*. 1999. http://po.pbs.org wgbh/amex/kids/civilrights/features_hutchison.html.

Richman, Irving Berdine. *Rhode Island, Its Making and Its Meaning*. New York: GP Putnam and Sons, 1902.

"Roger Williams: A Brief Biography." Roger Williams Family Association. 2015. www.rogerwilliams.org/biography.htm.

Winthrop, John. *Winthrop's Journal: History of New England, 1630–1649*, Edited by James Kendall Hosmer. New York: Charles Scribner's Sons, 1908.

Withey, Lynne. *Urban Growth in Colonial Rhode Island: Newport and Providence in the Eighteenth Century*. Albany, N.Y.: State University of New York Press, 1984.

Wright, Louis B. *The Cultural Life of the American Colonies*. New York: Harper Torchbooks, 1962.

Wright, Louis B. *Life in Colonial America*. New York: Capricorn Books, 1971.

Index